MW00883571

"In the name of Allah,
the Compassionate, the Merciful"

ISBN 978-1449917630

How to Use These Books

The Mini Tafseer Book Series is designed to teach children the Tafseer (exegesis) of all the suwaar (chapters) in the 30th Part of the Qur'aan. Each book in this 38 book series covers a different surah. The books feature:

- Special facts about the surah
- Arabic text of the surah
- English transliteration (to assist non-Arabic speakers)
- English translation
- Simplified Tafseer
- Illustrations/Coloring pages (no animals/humans)
- Highlighted Arabic vocabulary
- Sahih Ahadith
- One sentence summary of what the surah is about
- Review section
- Notes on the text (additional facts and information)

Teaching Tips:

If your younger child has trouble going through the whole book in one sitting, or does not retain all of the information taught, then just focus on the Tafseer pages first (i.e. those that explain the verses of the surah) and save the additional information contained in the Quick Facts, What's Special, Asbaab An-Noozool, and Vocabulary sections* for later when your child has mastered the Tafseer.

For older or advanced students who need more of a challenge, you can take time to go through all sections and discuss the lesson notes for that section (located at the end of the text). This will make lessons more challenging and provide a deeper understanding of the Tafseer, and Allah knows best.

*Some books may not contain all of these sections.

Mini Tafseer Book Series

Suratul-Hoomazah

Quick Facts About Suratul-Hoomazah...

Suratul-Hoomazah was
revealed in **Makkah**.

Suratul-Hoomazah tells us about things
that Allah does not want us to do like
talking about and making fun of others
and **not sharing our money**.

Suratul-Hoomazah gets its name from the
first verse where Allah talks about
"Hoo-ma-zah", the people who talk
about others.

So what is
Suratul-Hoomazah about?

Suratul-Hoomazah is about two sins that a lot of people do. They think these two sins are small, but they are VERY BIG!

1. **Talking about and making fun of people.**

2. **Not sharing your money with people who are in need.**

Allah tells us in Suratul-Hoomazah that the people who do these two sins are in BIG TROUBLE!

Now let's get ready to learn what Suratul-Hoomazah is all about!

We will start by learning **6 new words** from the Qur'aan.

The more words you know from the Qur'aan, the better you will understand each surah that you learn insha-Allah.

Understanding the Qur'aan is what Allah wants us to do!

So let's get started right now!

6 NEW WORDS!

Vocabulary List

Keep a look out for the following vocabulary words while you read! These words will help you remember the meaning of Suratul-Hoomazah, insha-Allah!

scorner

هُمَزَة

(hoo-ma-zah)

mocker

لُمَزَة

(loo-ma-zah)

gather/collect
(as in collecting money)

جَمَعَ

(ja-ma-'a)

his wealth/wealth

مَالاً/مَالَهُ

(maa-la-hoo/maa-lun)

no!
(It's not going to happen!)

كَلاَّ

(kal-laa)

The Crusher
(This is one of the names of the Hellfire)

ٱلْحُطَمَة

(al-hoo-ta-mah)

Now that we are ready,
we need to start the right way...

There are **two things** we should say before we start reading a surah from the Qur'aan, can you remember what they are?

Color in your numbers!

#1 We say the Isti'aadhah[1] ...

I seek refuge with Allah from the cursed Shaytaan.

('A-'oo-thoo-bil-laa-he-me-nash-shay-taa-nir-ra-jeem)

أَعُوذُ بِاللهِ مِنَ
الشَّيْطَانِ الرَّجِيمِ

We start reading Qur'aan by asking Allah to protect us from Shaytaan and...

#2 We say the Basmallah²...

In the name of Allah, the Entirely Merciful,
the Especially Merciful.

(Bis-mil-laa-hir-rah-maa-nir-ra-heem)

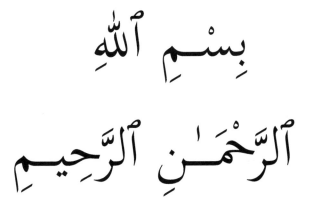

بِسْمِ ٱللهِ

ٱلرَّحْمَٰنِ ٱلرَّحِيمِ

We remember Allah and say how great He is for giving us so many wonderful blessings!

Okay!

We are ready to go now! You know your **new words** and you've said the **Isti'aadhah** and **Basmallah**...

Now it is time to learn what
Suratul-Hoomazah says...

"WOE unto every scorner and mocker!"

(Way-lool-lee-kool-lee hoo-ma-zah-til-loo-ma-zah)

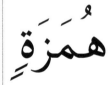 

Allah starts this surah by telling us about the first of two sins that He really, REALLY does not like...

Allah hates this sin so much that He revealed Suratul-Hoomazah to teach us **not to do it.**

This sin is the first thing Allah mentions in this surah (in the very first ayaat) before anything else.

Allah says that the people who do it are in **BIG TROUBLE** with Him.

It is easy to do, most people think it is very, very small, but it is one of the **biggest and ugliest sins in the world!**

It is a sin that many people will be punished for doing[3], it is...

Talking about people and making fun of them!

There are lots of ways to talk about others and make fun of them and <u>ALL</u> of them are included in the words **"Hoo-ma-zah"** and **"Loo-ma-zah"** used in the first ayah of Suratul-Hoomazah.

We can put all these types of talking about others and making fun of them into **three groups** [4]...

1. Mockery

2.Backbiting

3.Slander

What is Mockery?

Mockery is to do something with your <u>hands, eyes, or words</u> to make fun of someone.

Have you ever had someone **call you mean names or make fun of you**? Maybe they made fun of the way you dress, or the way you talk? Whenever someone makes fun of another person, saying things that the person does not like,
THAT IS MOCKERY!

Whenever a person **rolls their eyes, winks or gives looks** to show that they think another person has done something to laugh at (even if they do not say anything),
THAT IS MOCKERY!

Whenever a person uses their **hands** to make fun of another person (like putting their hands on their ears and flapping them like an elephant, to show that another person has big ears),
THAT IS MOCKERY!

Even if a person just watches others make fun of a person, and does not stop them,
THAT IS MOCKERY, TOO!

Has anyone ever **mocked** you?
Write what they said or did in the bubbles.
How did that make you feel?

Would you mock anyone now that you
know what a big sin it is?

What is Backbiting?

Backbiting is to talk about someone when the person is <u>not around</u>, saying things the person would not like said. [5]

Usually, people don't mean to backbite, but after they start talking with friends, it seems **more interesting** to add details about other people that might be funny, sad, or unbelievable.
THAT IS BACKBITING!

Whenever a person talks about someone using their **name** (so everyone knows whom we are talking about), in order to enjoy ourselves more, make others laugh, or criticize,
THAT IS BACKBITING!

Whenever a person **describes** what another person has done (even if they do not use the person's name) so that anyone can figure out whom they are talking about,
THAT IS BACKBITING!

Even if a person just listens to someone talking about others, and does not stop them,
THAT IS BACKBITING, TOO!

Have you ever had someone **backbite** you?
Write what they said in the bubbles.
How did that make you feel?

Would you backbite anyone now that you
know what a big sin it is?

What is Slander?

Slander is to say something about a person that is <u>not true</u> in order to make that person look bad. [6]

When a person tells other people something about another person that is **not true**,
THAT IS SLANDER!

When a person says something about another person that is a little true, but they **exaggerate** by making the story more interesting or funny,
THAT IS SLANDER!

When we talk to others about **rumors** (things we have heard from other people, but do not know for sure are true),
THAT IS SLANDER!

When a person sees someone do something and then tells others about it, acting as if they know for sure why or what a person was doing, when they really they do not know,
THAT IS SLANDER!

Even if a person just listens to other people slandering, and does not stop them,
THAT IS SLANDER, TOO!

Have you ever been **slandered**?
Write what they said in the bubbles.
How did that make you feel?

Would you slander anyone now that you
know what a big sin it is?

Why are mockery, backbiting & slander so bad?

They are so bad because they **hurt people** and Allah does not want us to harm anyone or be unfair.

Talking about and making fun of others is so bad that Allah and Rasulullahﷺ have told us that doing it is like...

Eating dead flesh!

Allah tells us in the Qur'aan...

"*Oh you who believe! Avoid suspicion as much (as possible): for suspicion in some cases is a sin: and spy not on each other behind their backs. Would any of you like to* **eat the flesh of his dead brother**? *No! you would hate it...but fear Allah, for Allah is Oft-Returning, Most Merciful.*"
(Qur'aan 49:12)

How can you make sure that you do not mock, backbite, or slander anyone?

Here are 10 tips to get you on the right track!

1. Don't say something about another person that they would **not like said.**

2. If you need to talk about another person for some reason (i.e. in order to teach a lesson, etc.) make sure you **never use the person's name.**

3. **Don't describe people** (how they look, where they live or work etc.) that would help others know who you are talking about.

4. **Don't exaggerate** (stretch the truth just to make people laugh or like your story more).

5. **Don't lie** and say something that is not true.

6. **Don't spread rumors** or any information that you have "heard" from others.

7. **Don't roll your eyes, wink, or give looks** to make fun of others.

8. **Don't call people names** (even nicknames for friends and family) that they do not like.

9. **Don't even listen** to others who are mocking, backbiting or slandering.

10. **Remind others about these rules** so they will not be mocking, backbiting, or slandering anyone either!

Are there times when we <u>have</u> to talk about other people?

There are only three times when a Muslim must talk about another person using their name, and even telling something about that person that they would not like said. Allah will not punish us in these **three cases**.

Partnerships

If someone asks you for information about a person they want to get married to, go into business with, or live next to, you are allowed to tell anything you know about that person (good or bad) in order to protect the questioner from harm.

Legal Matters

If you are a witness to a crime or you need to get a Fatwa (religious opinion) in order to know if something is allowed in Islaam, you can tell what you know (good or bad) to the police, lawyer, judge, and/or imam in order to stop bad actions and encourage good ones.

Warning against Harm

If there is a person who is dangerous, you can warn others not to listen to him. For example a person who is teaching incorrect information about Islaam or a person who steals money from his customers.

What if a person has already talked about others or made fun of them?

What can that person do to be forgiven? [7]

There are four things a person must do to be forgiven for talking about or making fun of others...

1. **Ask Allah for forgiveness and try never to do it again.** This will erase the sin you did in the past with good deeds that you do in the future.

2. **Ask the person you harmed to forgive you** (if they know what you said about them[8]). This will erase the bad feelings that person has towards you and replace them with good feelings.

3. **Make du'a to Allah to forgive you and the person you harmed.** This will erase your sins and replace them with good deeds.

4. **Say good things about the person to other people.** This will erase the bad thoughts people may have about the person, and replace them with good thoughts.

Let's review...

Allah has revealed Suratul-Hoomazah to tell us about **two big sins** that Allah does not want us to do.

We have learned all about the **first sin**...

We should never talk about or make fun of others by mocking, backbiting, or slandering!

Now let's learn about the second
big sin, can you guess what it is?
Turn the page to find out!

"Who collects wealth and (continuously) counts it."

(Al-la-thee ja-ma-'a maa-low-wa-'ad-da-dah)

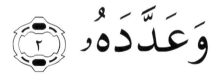

Allah tells us that the **second sin** He does not want us to do is something that people who mock, backbite, and slander like to do, too! The second sin is...

Miserliness

Miserliness is to keep all of your money for yourself, and not share it with others.

Misers do not think nicely about other people. That is why they do not share their money (they think no one else works as hard as they do, or is as smart at saving money as they are). Because of this, misers also mock, backbite, and slander other people too!

What a combination of two terrible sins!

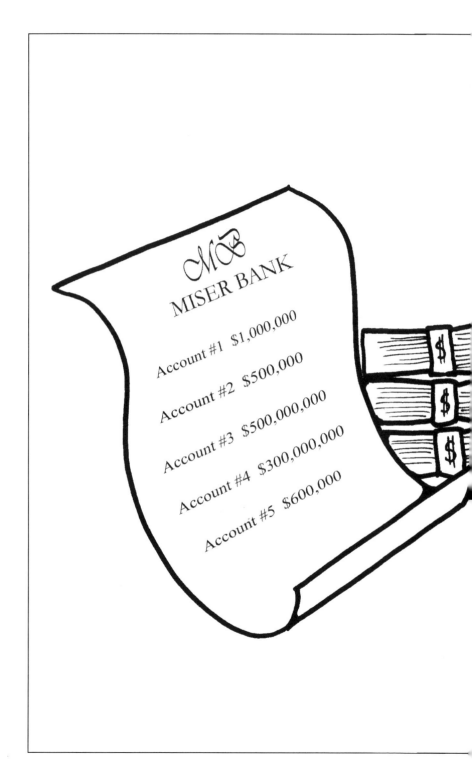

Allah does not just tell us that being a miser is bad; He describes what misers do, so we will know what it means to be a miser.

Allah tells us first that misers are always **counting their money**. They want to make sure they don't lose any of it, not one single penny!

They also enjoy counting their money because they like to see how much they have, and know when they have more than before.

Misers **worship money**, the money is more important to them then Allah, their family and friends, or anything else in this world.

The more they have the happier they are, and if they lose any (even the smallest amount) they get so angry that they will not be happy until they get it back with more on top.

But that's not all...

"He thinks that his wealth will make him live forever!"

(Yah-sa-boo an-na ma-la-hoo akh-la-dah)

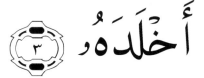

Misers love money so much, they think it will make them live forever!

They think that they can use their money to get the best **doctors and medicine** so they will not get sick or old.

They think they will build **huge monuments** for themselves, like the kings and pharaohs did, so that even if they die everyone will remember them and see how great they were.

But all their money will never stop them from dying and going back to Allah!

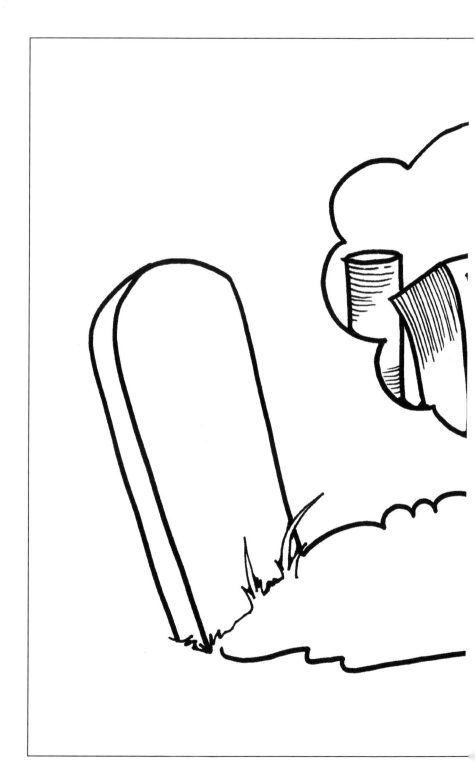

"No! He will surely be thrown into the Crusher!"

(Kal-la la-yoom-ba-than-na fil-hoo-ta-mah)

كَلَّا لَيُنْبَذَنَّ

فِي ٱلْحُطَمَةِ ﴿٤﴾

Mockers, backbiters, slanderers, and misers think that the things they do (like saving money, talking about and making fun of others) makes them important and better than everyone else, **but that is not true.**

They don't even think what they are doing is a sin, they think what they are doing is REALLY SMART, **but that is not true either!**

Allah tells us the truth about these people...

Allah says NO! Those people who talk about others or who do not share their money will be punished; they will be punished in...

Al-Hootamah

(The Crusher!)

"And what can make you know what is the Crusher?"

(Wa-maa ad-raa-ka mal-hoo-ta-mah)

وَمَآ أَدۡرَىٰكَ مَا

 ٱلۡحُطَمَةُ

But what is Al-Hootamah?

Allah tells us **4 things** about Al-Hootamah in this surah...

"It is the fire of Allah, (eternally) fuelled..."

(Na-rool-la-hil-moo-qa-dah)

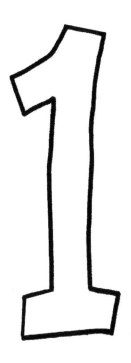

Allah's very hottest fire...

Al-Hootamah is a fire that Allah has made as a punishment for the people who talk about and make fun of others and do not share their money.

He has made it the **very hottest fire** just for them...

"…which will rise directed at the hearts…"

(Al-la-tee tat-ta-lee'oo 'a-lal-af-ee-dah)

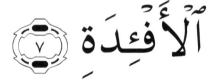

Rises up over them...

The fire of Al-Hootamah will **rise up over** them. In their hearts, the people will be so scared, but it will not make any difference. The punishment will come over and over again and it will not stop. They will not die or be able to get out of the punishment at all...

"Indeed, it will be closed down upon them…"

(ln-na-ha 'a-lay-him moo'-sa-dah)

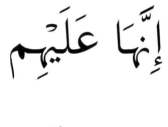

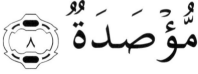

No escape...

Al-Hootamah **will be completely closed.**
There will be no opening or way to get
out. Like a safe that has been locked
with a heavy door and deadbolt, there
will be no way to escape...

"…in extended columns!"

(Fee 'a-ma-din moo-mad-da-dah)

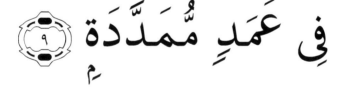

فِي عَمَدٍ مُّمَدَّدَةٍ ⟨٩⟩

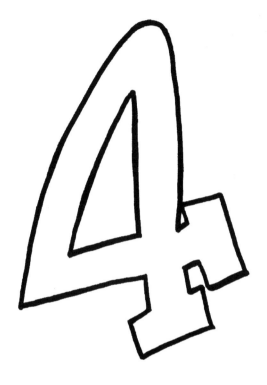

Columns...

Al-Hootamah has **tall columns** that will keep the mockers, backbiters, slanderers, and misers inside. These columns are very strong and very big.

So, what is Suratul-Hoomazah about?

Suratul-Hoomazah tells us about two sins that Allah hates...

Talking about and making fun of others
&
Not sharing money

Suratul-Hoomazah also tells us four things about Al-Hootamah (Jahannam)...

It is Allah's very hottest fire,
it rises up and over the sinners,
it has no escape, and
it has strong columns.

The End!

Suratul-Hoomazah Review

What is Suratul-Hoomazah about?

It is about two sins that Allah hates, talking about and making fun of others, and not sharing money.

In what city was Suratul-Hoomazah revealed?

Makkah

What does Suratul-Hoomazah get its name from?

The first ayah that talks about "Hoomazah", the backbiters.

What is the first sin that Allah mentions in this surah?

Talking about and making fun of others.

What are the three main ways that people talk about and make fun of others?

Mockery, backbiting, & slander.

 What is mockery?

Mockery is to do something with your <u>hands, eyes, or words</u> to make fun of someone.

 What is backbiting?

Backbiting is to talk about someone when the person is <u>not around</u>, saying things the person would not like said.

 What is slander?

Slander is to say something about a person that is <u>not true</u> in order to make that person look bad.

 What if you just listen to others mocking, backbiting and slandering, is that still a sin?

Yes, it is a sin if you listen and do not stop them.

Why is talking about and making fun of others so bad?

Because it hurts people and Allah does not want us to harm anyone or be unfair.

What did Allah and Rasulullahﷺ say that mockery, backbiting, and slander was like?

It is like eating dead flesh.

What are the 10 tips to keep ourselves from mocking, backbiting & slandering?

See page 31 for the complete list.

What are the 3 times when we can talk about others?

1. Partnerships
2. Legal Matters
3. Warning against harm

What are the four things we need to do to be forgiven for talking about and making fun of others?

1. Ask Allah for forgiveness and try never to do it again.

2. Ask the person you harmed to forgive you (if they know what you said).

3. Make du'a to Allah to forgive you and the person you harmed.

4. Say good things about the person to other people.

 What is the second sin mentioned in this surah that Allah hates?

Miserliness

 What are the signs of a miser?

1. He counts his money all the time.
2. He thinks his money will make him live forever.

 Is what the miser thinks true?

No

What is the truth about misers?

Allah will send them, along with those who talk about and make fun of others, to Al-Hootamah.

What is Al-Hootamah?

It is the part of Jahannam for people who talk about and make fun of others, and do not share their money.

What are the four things Allah tells us about Al-Hootamah?

1. It is Allah's fire, the very hottest part.

2. It rises up over the sinners.

3. It is closed; there are no openings.

4. It has columns that keep the sinners inside.

Matching

Directions: Draw a line to match each description on the right with the word it describes on the left. Answers are in the following page.

Mockery

Keeping all your money for yourself.

Backbiting

Telling lies about people to make them look bad.

Slander

Saying things about someone when they are not around (even if what you say is true).

Miserliness

Making fun of someone with your eyes, hands or words.

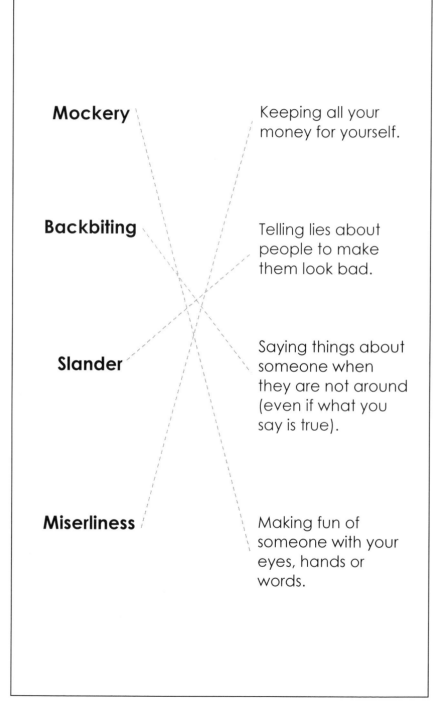

Mockery

Backbiting

Slander

Miserliness

Keeping all your money for yourself.

Telling lies about people to make them look bad.

Saying things about someone when they are not around (even if what you say is true).

Making fun of someone with your eyes, hands or words.

Matching

Directions: Draw a line to match each statement on the right with the word that defines it on the left. Be careful, one statement is not bad to say; circle it when you find it. Answers are in the following page.

Mockery

> Hameed winked at his friend and smiled when Layla walked by and tripped on a rock.

Backbiting

> "I am sure it was Adam I saw stealing money from the donation box. He had a dollar in his hand when he walked away!"

Slander

> "Grandma is sick with the flu so we need to make soup for her."

Miserliness

> "I will not give you money to pay for medicine, you always waste my money on things you do not really need!"

> "Rayan has the worst temper, she is always yelling!"

Mockery - - - - - - - - -

Hameed winked at his friend and smiled when Layla walked by and tripped on a rock.

Backbiting

"I am sure it was Adam I saw stealing money from the donation box. He had a dollar in his hand when he walked away!"

Slander

"Grandma is sick with the flu so we need to make soup for her."

"I will not give you money to pay for medicine, you always waste my money on things you do not really need!"

Miserliness

"Rayan has the worst temper, she is always yelling!"

Notes to the text

[1] Allah has said that we should seek refuge with Him from Shaytaan before reciting Qur'aan by saying, "A-oo-thoo-bill-laa-he-min-nash-shay-taan-nir-ra-jeem".

(So when you) want to recite the Qur'an, seek refuge with Allah from Shaytaan, the outcast (the cursed one). (Qur'aan 16:98)

The majority of scholars state that reciting this phrase, known as the Isti'aathah in Arabic (pronounced Is-ti-`aa-thah), is recommended and not required, and therefore, not reciting it does not constitute a sin. However, Rasulullah ﷺ always said the Isti`aathah. In addition, the Isti`aathah wards off the evil of Shaytaan, which is necessary; the rule is that the means needed to implement a requirement of the religion is itself also required. And when one says, "I seek refuge with Allah from the cursed devil." Then this will suffice.
(Tafseer Ibn Kathir)

[2] Saying the Basmallah, "Bis-mil-laa-hir-rah-maa-nir-ra-heem" before reciting any surah, except for the ninth, Suratut-Towba, which does not have the Basmallah in the beginning, is agreed upon by all scholars past and present.

[3] In addition to the punishment discussed in Suratul-Hoomazah for those who mock, backbite,

and slander, there are other punishments mentioned for these crimes that are detailed in the ahadith (see below). The existence of more than one punishment for a specific sin does not indicate a contradiction or error in the Qur'aan and ahadith, rather it indicates that the sinners will receive multiple punishments; some will occur in this life, some in the grave, and some in the hereafter, and Allah knows best.

It was narrated that Ibn Abbaas said: The Messenger of Allah ﷺ passed by two graves and said, "They are being punished, but they are not being punished for anything that was difficult to avoid. One of them used to walk about spreading malicious gossip (nameemah), and the other used not to take precautions to avoid getting urine on himself when he urinated." Then he called for a green branch, which he split in two and planted a piece on each grave, and said, "May their torment be reduced so long as these do not dry out."
(Sahih Al-Bukhari and Sahih Muslim)

4 There are a variety of opinions as to the exact meaning of "Hoomazah" and "Loomazah". They have been translated as "scorner" and "mocker" respectively. However, there are several other interpretations given by the scholars of tafseer that we will list on the next page for reference.

What we can understand from all the interpretations is that "Hoomazah" and

"Loomazah" include any kind of disrespectful and humiliating treatment of others.

However, in order to make this concept clear for children we have grouped such behavior into three general categories (mocking, backbiting & slander) and Allah knows best.

Hoomazah	Loomazah
Those who use innuendo with their eyes and hands to insult others	Those who use their tongue to insult others
Finding fault with someone in front of them	Finding fault with someone behind their back
Apparent fault-finding	Subtle fault-finding done with the eyebrows and hands
Defaming by using low titles/name calling	Defaming by using low titles/name calling

[5] *It was narrated from Abu Hurayrah that the Messenger of Allah ﷺ said, "Do you know what gheebah (backbiting) is?" They said, "Allah and His Messenger know best." He said, "Saying something about your brother that he dislikes." It was said, "What if what I say about my brother is true?" He said, "If what you say is true then you have backbitten about him, and if it is not true,*

then you have slandered him."
(Sahih Muslim)

6 See note #5

7 The Prophet ﷺ said, *"Whoever has wronged his brother with regard to his honor or something, let him <u>ask him for forgiveness</u> before the time when there will be neither dinar nor dirham (money to pay off ones debts with), and if he has any good deeds it will be taken from him in proportion to the wrong he did, and if he does not have any good deeds (hasanaat), some of the other person's evil deeds (sayi'aat) will be taken and given to him (the sinner) to bear."* (Sahih Al-Bukhaari)

8 If the person whom you have mocked or slandered is unaware of what you have said some scholars, not all, allow that you do not need to tell the person what you have done, as this may cause more harm than good. Instead you can repent to Allah, and then speak well of the person or do some other good for the person to make up for the harm you have done, and Allah knows best.

Bibliography

1. Tafseer Ibn Kathir (Abridged), English translation by Shaykh Safiur-Rahman Al-Mubarakpuri, Darussalam Publishers, 2000

2. Sahih Al-Bukhari, English translation by Dr. Muhammed Muhsin Khan, Islamic University, Al-Medina Al-Munawwara, Kazi Publications, 1986

3. Sahih Muslim, English translation by Abdul Hamid Siddiqi, Shaykh Muhammad Ashraf Publishers, 1990

4. The Qur'aan (English translation), Saheeh International, Almunatada Alislami, Abul Qasim Publishing House, 1997

More Products Offered by Ad-Duha!

Ad-Duha is <u>not</u> just a bookstore, we offer complete curriculum packages for use by **homeschoolers or Islamic Schools.**

Our courses contain everything needed to teach in a home or classroom environment including:

- Daily Lesson Manuals
- Full-color, illustrated textbooks (no images of humans/animals)
- Activity filled workbooks
- Audiovisual software (no music or images of humans/animals)
- Enrichment activities for every subject and lesson
- Suggested field trips
- Integrated worksheets to reinforce lesson objectives
- Grading sheets
- Test preparation guides...and much more!

To get **free downloadable samples** of all our books and lesson manuals visit our web site at...

www.ad-duha.org

Made in the USA
Columbia, SC
06 September 2018